T0146640

Dog Breeding Secrets

Marcus E Curtis

authorHOUSE®

AuthorHouse™
1663 Liberty Drive
Bloomington, IN 47403
www.authorhouse.com
Phone: 1 (800) 839-8640

Published by AuthorHouse 09/18/2017

ISBN: 978-1-5462-0371-1 (sc)
ISBN: 978-1-5462-0369-8 (hc)
ISBN: 978-1-5462-0370-4 (e)

Library of Congress Control Number: 2017912335

Print information available on the last page.

This book is printed on acid-free paper.

Testimonials

We recommend this GREAT book to anyone who has ever been interested in learning both the basic and the intricate measures taken to becoming a reputable breeder. Marcus is a plethora of knowledge on the subject and we were so excited when we learned he was going to share that knowledge with the rest of us. It's a must read! Thankyou so much for your help and support Marcus and Yvette Curtis. We value your friendship dearly.

– Jay and Rebecca Howser.

Dark Mountain Mastiffs

After working in close range with Marcus while creating his book, we have not only learned tons of new information about dogs and dog breeding, but have also found a new love and respect for the newly re created breed, the stunningly beautiful American Mollosus. We are looking forward to watching this gorgeous breed mature and are also very excited to see how many people are going to benefit from having a gem like this in their private library at home.

– 818 Concepts

Two years ago I began to search for the best breeder I could find for a specific breed of dog. My research and findings led me to Marcus Curtis based out of California, I was in New Jersey. I had some initial trepidation working with a breeder that was so far away. However, I was quickly put at ease. The level of professionalism that Marcus exhibits in his business, also shows in his quality of breeding. Marcus has provided me with two dogs of the highest standard I could ask for. The dogs are well mannered, and the lineage is carefully and methodically chosen. I am excited that he is sharing his secrets with the world as his animals are some of the finest that I have ever owned.

– Joseph Amabile ,VP Artisan Manufacturing

Lead Vocalist- babyfacefinsterband.com

For many years my husband and I thought about getting a Neapolitan Mastiff. I began my search and discovered that there are many types of breeders with very different looking dogs. After finding and talking with Marcus Curtis of Old World Mastinos I knew I had found the right one for us. He had beautiful dogs but that wasn't the most compelling reason we chose him. He was so passionate about breeding healthy dogs. He truly loved the breed and was only interested in improving it not milling it. We absolutely love our Old World Cleopatra, sister to Don Vito. She is an incredible dog and perfect for our family. Marcus is patient, methodical and above all else honest about his dogs. I know that he will protect and improve all his dogs and only allow them to go to appropriate homes. I am so honored to have one of his Neapolitan Mastiffs. I love following his well deserved success and I know that his positive and persistent nature will continue to bring him and others great joy. Marcus Curtis of Old World Mastinos will forever be known for his contributions to the Mastiff breeds.

– Daria Knowles

Testimonial about my personal experience with Marcus E. Curtis of Old World Mastinos.

Before I say anything about Marcus I would like to give some background information about myself.

My name is Felice Napolitano of Di Napoli Mastini, I grew up in Italy, My first experience with Mastini was 35 years ago with a gentleman named Zi Mimi´. I was a 10 years old boy sitting in his yard in Casamarciano Italy with many of many of the most famous Breeders of today which refer to him as the legend of Mastini, his nickname was O´ re´ dei cani" the king of the dogs. I was hooked on the breed then, as a young adult I moved to the greatest country "USA" and didn't leave my passion behind. I started working with Vincenzo Manna of DSV kennel, Michele De Falco from Del Nolano, Patrizio Italia Della Grotta Azzurra, Giuliano del Gheno from Del Gheno Kennel and many other. I owned many dogs offspring of the greatest dogs breed: Carnera Della Azzurra, litter mate of LION DVS the first top dog produced by DSV, Gennarino DSV, Peppiniello DSV, Leone DSV and many many other.

I'm not name dropping but I'm trying to get a point across.

The people named above have the same passion, tenacity and a dream to get the Mastino of the 80 to the mastino of today. They did whatever it took to achieve that goal never giving up through victory and defeats. I have been breeding Mastini in the USA for the past 26 years and a few years go started working with Marcus, together we produced some outstanding dogs but that isn't the important part of my experience with Marcus.

After the first few encounter and long phone calls I noticed something that I had not seen with many breeders in the USA in years. I felt his Passion for the Breed, his Tenacity and get ready A DREAM.

Wow I had not heard that word in many years, he not only wanted to better the Neapolitan mastiff breed but had a dream to create a better breed similar in looks but healthier, stronger and bigger.

Over the years her has never stopped we had many conversation about this new great breed and finally in mid 2017 he had the first litter of the AMERICAN MOLOSSUS. I thought to myself wow this guy is the most determined person in the breed I have met so far. This doesn't describe all of his quality, he has personally helped me many time without hesitation or a secret agenda and I know for sure of many other breeder that have received help with knowledge or a stud dog or help placing their dog if they met his top standard. I would like to conclude with this; Marcus and his wife are top class people in their personal life and business and I can guarantee you in writing as I'm doing now that if I will ever need to recommend a breeder Marcus of Old World Mastinos will be my first choice.

– Felice Napolitano

Di Napoli Mastini

Your thoughts are the architects of your destiny

-David O. McKay

THE DON

Old World Perseus

Old World Bane

Old World Sheeba

Old World Rosina 2.5 years

Old World Ren

Preface

The secrets of dog breeding - What are the secrets of dog breeding? It's a fascinating question. It's probably the reason you purchased this book! It's important to know these secrets if you are to pursue dog breeding, and the secrets are what everyone must seek, in any endeavor, to become great at what they decide to do. The secrets for general application are revealed in the quotes by successful people at the opening of each chapter. Don't skip them! The body of each chapter offers facts and very helpful tips specific to dog breeding: how it is done, why it is done, when it is done, and should it be done. These tailored secrets were gleaned over a 20 year span of dog breeding experience, observation of multiple successful breeders, mentorship, apprenticeship, and through reading numerous books on the subject.

My goals are to give you a great tool to help you understand dog breeding, to help you develop a healthy dog breeder's mindset, to instruct you on why it's been done for thousands of years and, finally, to encourage a decision: should you do it yourself. It was also designed to be a template for you to apply as a positive approach for other endeavors in life. This reference guide contains useful information, multiple pictures, and historical quotes for you to enjoy while you're reading. I truly hope you benefit from this book now, and refer to it often for many years to come.

Chapter 1

What's your Purpose

My wife Yvette and "THE DON" Champion Old World Don Vito

Old World Ren at 7 months

My wife Yvette and Old World Ice Cube at 6 weeks

Old World pups at 5 weeks with Devon and Maleaha

Efforts and courage are not enough without purpose
and courage

-John F Kennedy

What is your purpose? It is the most important question everyone should ask before they commit to something. This book is written for you. It is a guide to help you understand the breeding process, what is involved, how to prepare, what to expect (good and bad) and what it takes. I decided to write this book so that it could be an entertaining way for you to reach a decision to breed, or not to breed, dogs. If nothing else, my intent is to help you, in a simple, direct way, to learn about dog breeding and what challenges dog breeders face. I'm confident, as well, that you will learn tried and true practices about setting and achieving goals that can positively influence all your life decisions.

Purpose-the reason for which something is done or created or for which something exists:

I ask you to start with the question, "Why?" Why have you considered dog breeding? Why are you currently breeding dogs? Why haven't you considered dog breeding? Why have you not progressed in your dog breeding? "Why" is the biggest question you can ask yourself in anything you do in life. Dog breeding is no exception! Ask yourself these questions, as they pertain to you, and define your purpose. Educate yourself on the particular breed that interests you. Learn the written standard. Go visit dog shows. Research dog breeders who have produced Champion dogs. Look at pictures and videos of dogs in different breeding programs and see the progression or regression over a period of time. See for yourself what defines greatness within your chosen breed and how it affects you.

IT Champion Brigante Del Castellaccio bred by Salvatore Scherma

Ed Shepherd and I

You see, to me, breeding is an Art. It is a highly trained skill, and to be able to breed it takes drive, passion, desire and emotion. It is no easy task, and to be successful you must have definitive purpose. You must visualize what you perceive as perfection and have a drive and a white fire-like passion to have that vision materialize.

THE DON at Bark in the Park

There are a number of important questions to consider. Is your chosen breed hale and hearty, or does it have a history of delicate health or ailments? Can you expect good fertility rates, producing consistently? How important is intelligence? What is required of the breed in temperament? What is perceived as good construction and correct movement? What is acceptable longevity? Is the line an inbred, line bred, back bred or outcrossed dog? The answers to these questions will have an impact on the outcome of your decision and aid you in evaluating the pros and cons regarding the breed. You will be better equipped to decide whether or not you should breed. Answering these types of questions will help you determine what your purpose is in the breed; the "why." Should you be a fan, fancier, owner, one-time breeder or career breeder?

Great breeding results, as with any life work, will require a great deal of sacrifice, dedication, hard work and a tremendous amount of focused effort. If you love what you do, and if you have a measurable goal, you will achieve what you set out to do. The sacrifice, dedication, hard work and effort won't seem as difficult. A goal is key. The standard is the goal. So you must decide if what you have to work with is at, above or below the standard and why.

1/3

2/3 LENGTH OF HEAD

Old World Mastinos

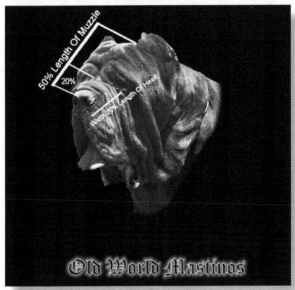

50% Length Of Muzzle

20%

Width 20% Length Of Head

Old World Mastinos

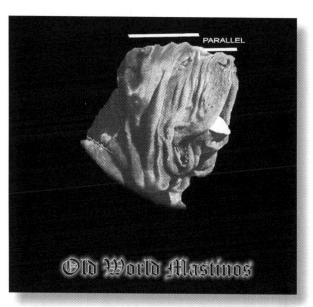

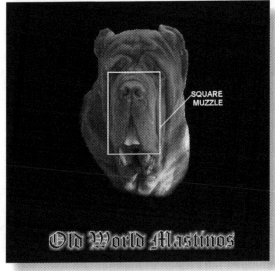

Consider the pair you are going to breed. Are they going to help you get to the standard or improve? Are they healthy? What features and characteristics do they have, compared to the standard or your desired results? Does the pair build on strengths and improve on weakness? These are questions you should ask yourself when deciding if you should breed or how you should move forward in your breeding program.

Chapter 2

Dogs Anatomy

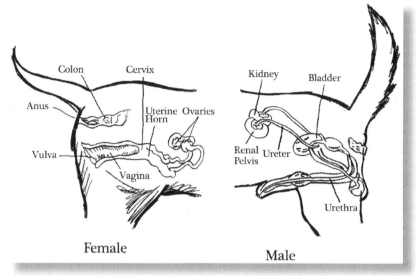

Female   Male

Art work by 818 Concepts

Chapter 3

Breeding Types

Yvette with Old World Perseus and Mlm's Old World Amara

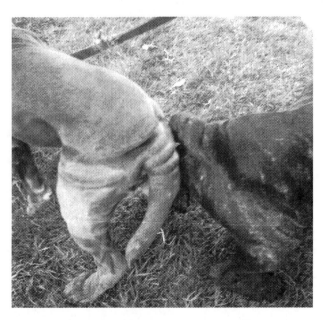

Old World Perseus and Mlm's Old World Amara

The first step towards getting somewhere is to decide that you are not going to stay where you are

-J.P. Morgan

In breeding, line breeding, back breeding and out crossing

Knowing the difference in breeding selection is very important. Breeding by selection is an Art and should not be taken lightly. Although different breeders may have varying opinions, I believe there are 5 types of breeding: inbreeding, line breeding, back breeding, outcrossing and breed crossing.

Inbreeding is the breeding of super closely related dogs such as brother/sister, granddaughter to grandsire, grandson to grandmother, niece to uncle, nephew to aunt or half brother to half sister.

Old World Bonnie Parker at 6 weeks

Old World Bonnie Parker

Line breeding is the breeding of dogs with related blood within 3-5 generations.

Maya with Old World Bonnie Parker

Old World Ice Cube at 7 months

Back breeding is the breeding of mother to son, father to daughter.

Outcrossing is the breeding of dogs that have no blood relationship within 5 generations. Out crossing can be very useful in bringing in a new bloodline, increasing the gene pool, increasing some new characteristics to a particular line such as physical aesthetics or looks, health, intelligence, temperament, fertility, coat, movement and drive.

Old World Santino at 2 weeks being held

Old World Santino at 9.5 weeks

Breed crossing is the breeding of two different breeds. This has been done to create virtually all breeds, as well as to change a breed, introduce new genes, improve movement, increase or decrease size, alter temperament, altar coat, color etc. All breeds are products of breed crossing at some point. The only 3 original dogs were wolves, Dingoes and the African wild dog.

American Molossus pup Old World Sasquatch at 7 weeks and I

Old World Euphrates at 8 weeks

Chapter 4

Paring by Design

Carnera with breeder Pepe Siano and Patrizio Vitale

Carnera Della Grotta Azzurra

Choice, not circumstances, determines your success

-Anonymous

In my opinion, next to your knowing your purpose and the "why," this may be the most important chapter. Paring by design is truly the Art of breeding. When selecting a pair for breeding, you must literally understand your particular breed inside and out. You should educate yourself on everything there is to know about that breed from the outer appearance, muzzle to the tail, as well as their function, temperament, construction, movement, behaviors etc. Why was the breed created in the first place? The aesthetics, or appearance, outlined in the written standard is important to know so you can compare your sire and dam to that model. The criterion for judging includes the head, style of head, proportions, head planes, the muzzle, dentition, eye setting, expression, ear setting, nose, nostrils, lips, construction of the skull, eye color, gum color, neck, shoulders, chest, insertion of the shoulders, depth of chest, leg position, joints, paws, toes, claws and color, positioning of the paws, loin, topline, tail setting, hock, thighs, rear, size and color. Becoming knowledgeable of your breed will enable you to evaluate the pair you've selected by referring to the set standards.

Chapter 5

When To Breed

You don't have to swing hard to hit a home run. If you got the timing, it'll go

-Yogi Berra

Deciding when to breed is a decision that's up to only you. Factors to consider are the age of the dam, genetics, and hormones. Healthy females, in general, will have a cycle (go into heat) approximately every 6 months. There are times when females have only one heat a year and some have silent heats. The best way to know when a dog is in heat is by visual observation and examination. Generally, the vulva will swell and then blood will drip from the vulva. Sometimes there will be just spotting, but other times there will be a pretty heavy flow. When this happens, immediately mark your calendar and keep a journal or folder to record this data for future reference. Most females will be ready to be bred between 6-18 days after the show of blood. If your female's vulva is swollen but you see no blood you can either gently insert a swab or Q-tip to check for blood, or go to a licensed veterinarian. Once day 1 is established, you can count the days and observe her behavior and vulva daily. When she gets closer to the optimum breeding time, the blood starts to lighten to a pink color and then clear. Most females will then let the male know she's ready by moving her tail to the side as they approach, which is known as flagging. Some females can be quite aggressive, backing up and flagging to her desired sire, while others will not act interested and can be irritable. These are the physical signs that your bitch may be ready to be bred.

Another approach is through the scientific method, taking the bitch into a Veterinarian and having blood drawn to check her progesterone levels. This is a very accurate way of determining the actual day the breeding should take place. Breedings are very important and timing is of the essence. Nature waits on no one so be prepared. Know the signs and do what is needed to ensure you have the timing right.

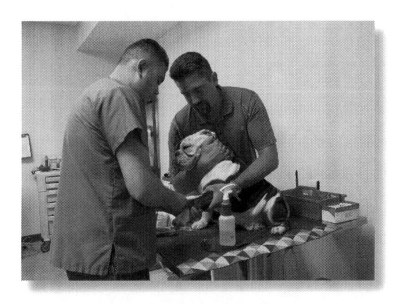

Chapter 6

How To Breed Step-By-Step

A journey of a thousand miles must begin with a single step

-Loa Tzu

Once you've gone through the process of examining your bitch, determined she is ready to be bred by counting the days and seeing her flag, or by doing the necessary bloodwork to determine when she should be bred, here are some step-by-step tips for how to breed.

There are 4 different methods of breeding dogs

1. The first is a natural breeding, where two dogs are bred at the optimal time, naturally, as nature intended. In cases of exotic breeds or large breeds, this method sometime requires help by one or more people. Whether on their own, or with assistance, the dogs must complete

what's called a tie to be successful. A tie occurs when the male's penis has been inserted, and the ball has swelled inside the female, causing them to be locked together, or tied. This tie can be 5 minutes to as long as an hour, depending on the dogs. This is the original and oldest method of dog breeding.

2. The second type of dog breeding is performing an AI, or artificial insemination. In this method the breeder collects semen from a dog manually and uses a syringe and pipette to inject the fresh semen into the bitch, with the goal of reaching the cervix. A breeder would purchase an AI kit containing rubber gloves, lubricant, alcohol swab, syringe, pipette and collection bag to perform this method.

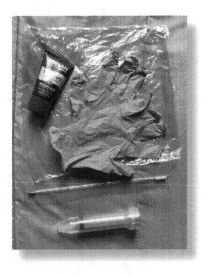

3. The third method of dog breeding is a TI, trans cervical insemination. This must be performed by a licensed veterinarian and a reproductive specialist. This method is similar to an AI, however, it is performed by a reproductive specialist using a very sophisticated machine that can insert the injection tube much further and inflate it to hold the semen in. The procedure is performed while being viewed by a camera. This method is very effective and the percentage rate of success is higher than the AI. The drawbacks to this method are that very few Vets perform the procedure, and the bitch must be able to stay still for an extended period of time, which can be quite difficult.

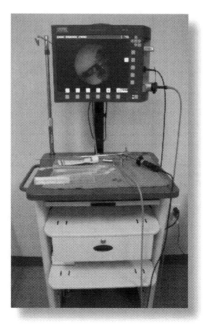

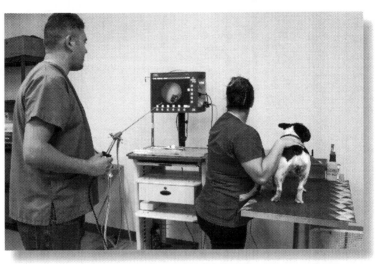

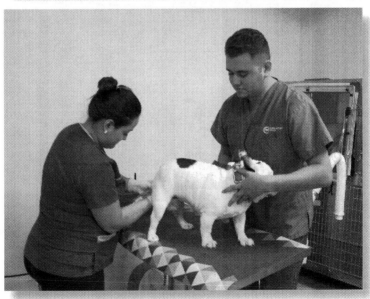

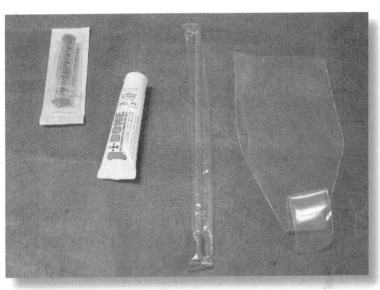

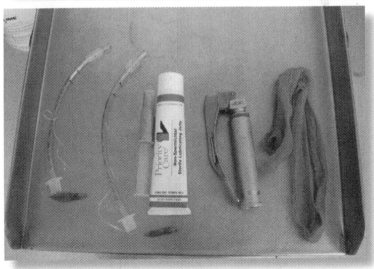

4. The fourth and final method, with the highest success rate, is surgical insemination. A licensed reproductive veterinarian makes a small incision on the bitch, right above her uterus and places the semen directly onto the eggs, distributing it evenly in both ducts. This procedure is done surgically, using a camera for precise accuracy. Research shows this method has the highest percentage rate of success, 97-99%, of the 4 methods. The downside to this method is similar to the TI. Very few Vets perform the procedure, and it can be quite expensive, also.

Some final notes:

- if you are considering breeding dogs, get is much information you can first
- make sure you have consulted experienced breeders for mentorship
- never try performing any of these methods without knowing all the pros and cons of dog breeding

- o dog health, basic reproduction, knowing about prenatal care of the bitch and whelping
- o the extreme costs of this endeavor.

Dog breeding should be left to experienced dog breeders, but now you know some basics of the four common methods of dog breeding.

Chapter 7

On the Clock

Life is about timing

-Carl Lewis

If you're a breeder, considering dog breeding, or want to understand the dog breeding process, one thing you must understand is you're on the clock. Nature waits for no one, and this is very important for many reasons. Understanding timing means that you must be available to drop what you're doing, or prepare to be flexible to the needs breed dogs. Females go into estrus on average twice a year. So, if you've gone down the checklist and you've determined the pair that's right, healthy, and paired for improvement, you'll need to know when she comes into heat/season.

Have a calendar, or chart, and document when your female comes into her first heat. Then document her next, which should be in approximately 6 months. I do not recommend breeding any female until at least her second or third heat. If you are careful, organized, and have documented her heat cycles, you'll be prepared for when she is ready to be bred.

Once a female goes into estrus, which means her vulva has swelled and blood is apparent, you must count the days.

Again, you're on the clock, so you cannot miss any days. Average females are ready to mate around day 12, but having blood work done to check her progesterone levels will tell you precisely what day will be the optimum day for breeding. I suggest the first bloodwork be done on day 7-8. The reason I suggest days 7-8 is because you must account for human error and a female that is irregular. Perhaps you missed a few days, or perhaps this female ovulates sooner than normal. Either way, be prepared, and increase your chances of success.

Once you've documented, prepared, tested and have bred her, you're still on the clock. The next date to prepare for is 34 days from the date of insemination or natural breeding, to have a licensed veterinarian perform an ultrasound, then day 55, if you decide to do an X-ray. Each is effective at determining pregnancy and can also help determine how many pups she is carrying.

The next date that should be marked on your calendar is

day 60 from the breeding or insemination date. This is the day you must start monitoring the dog for a natural birth or determine that your female will be having a C-Section. Most females give birth days 60-63.

Understand, you are on the clock from the time you decide to become a dog breeder, tracking, recording, and calendaring.

Although dog breeding can be a wonderful and rewarding occupation or hobby, it takes a great deal of dedication and consideration if one is to become successful. Vacations, getaways and work can be severely impacted by the dogs timing. You need to consider you will need to be available when the female comes into heat, when she must have testing done, when she must be bred, when she needs ultrasounds and/or X-ray's, when the female needs to be taken in for a C Section or for natural whelping. You will be tracking and recording for months afterward for puppy care and nurturing. All of these timelines are crucial and must be adhered to.

If you understand you're on the clock, embrace it with a positive mental attitude, and are calculated, organized and prepared, congratulations, you've put yourself in a great position for success!

Chapter 8

The Big Day and Sleepless Nights

(portions of this chapter were taken from article Whelping and
raising puppies Written by MistyTrails Havanese)

Amara 2 days out

It's hard to beat a person who never gives up

-Babe Ruth

Well, if you decided to be a breeder, you've selected the right pair, paired by design, you've followed the correct steps to know when to breed, completed the breeding and its confirmed, then well done, the big day is soon to follow.

What is the big The Big Day? The big day you've been waiting and preparing for. It's the birthday day of your beautiful puppies. It's the first day of life and a wonderful moment that took so much time, preparation, work and due diligence to make happen.

On this day a natural birth can take place, or a Cesarean Section birth can take place. There are pros and cons to both, but both can be a success.

A natural birth is where the bitch gives birth naturally and can be delivered with assistance by an experienced breeder. This is not uncommon, but the size of the puppies and the physical condition of the bitch can complicate a natural birth. The bitch can tire and quit pushing during delivery, a puppy can get stuck in the birth canal, and in rare occasions, the bitch can go into shock. Having experience and doing research will help you be prepared, should any of those situations arise.

The upside to a natural birth is, it's natural! Neither the mother nor her pups will have medication in their systems. Another positive aspect is that the dam is aware of the birth and will bond with her whelps more quickly and perhaps form a closer bond as well.

Cesarian/ C-Section

This is done for multiple reasons. In the larger breeds and Bully breeds, the procedure is done to avoid the risk of the puppies getting stuck during the birthing process. This can cause injury and even death, in some cases, to both the puppies and even the mother. Some dogs that have been bred with larger heads are more prone to these problems as are larger breeds, due to tiring.

If your gut tells you the natural birth is not progressing normally, as you envisioned a normal delivery, seek veterinary advice or take your bitch in to a vet ASAP. To avoid puppy deaths, you must work aggressively with your vet at the first sign of labor problems. I always advise people to go with how you feel, or simply schedule the C Section between days 60-63.

Why do a Cesarean?

The puppies might not be deliverable for various reasons, including puppy size, puppy head size, pelvic size, bad position of a puppy or puppies. Signs of puppy distress may force a quick decision to perform a C-section. Some signs of puppy stress can include red, dark red, black and or green discharge. Why is this important? This can mean that the placenta has detached, or there is fecal discharge.

A C-section should be performed no sooner than day 60, unless it becomes an emergency situation. Always delay the procedure as long as possible for puppy development and health.

Keep in mind, a C-section can be a good thing. It can be the safer thing to do and can be the overall best thing for your bitch, you and the vet.

Prep before surgery, the bitch should be clean and the vet will do another cleansing before surgery.

The vet will make an incision from the pubis to the umbilicus. In some cases with large puppies such as Neapolitan Mastiffs and American Molossus, and when the uterus is really long, the incision may need to be extended.

The bitch will usually be well covered and kept warm.

The uterine horns are then pulled out.

To allow fast removal of the puppies, an incision is made in the uterus. Most vets will have trained staff there throughout the procedure to assist.

Provided there were no complications, once the procedure is complete, all pups are removed, cleaned and warmed, the mother's milk should flow normally. She should be ready to take care of her babies once the anesthesia wears off.

C-Sections do not affect future breedings.

The insides of a dam after a C-section.

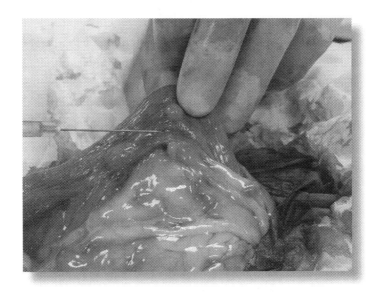

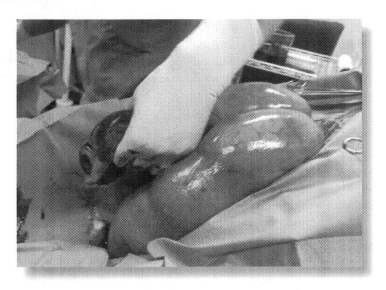

When the pups are retrieved, start to breathe and cry, it is an

exciting and rewarding moment for the vet and their staff.

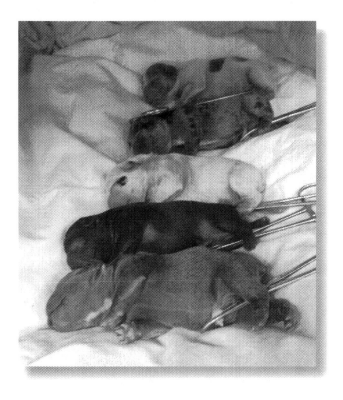

Pups in the warming box

After pups are delivered they are put in a warm box and your bitch is brought out. This is the time to have your newborn pups start to nurse. This helps stimulate her hormones, as well as see if she will need an injection of oxytocin to induce more production of milk. If all is well, she and the pups are ready to go home.

American Molossus pups just born

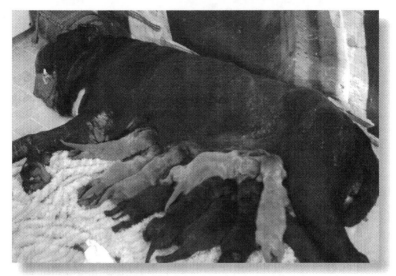

Old World Pandora and her pups

Old World Bane x Old World Sheeba pups at 5 days old

Chapter 9

Special Delivery - Prepping
To Sell And Place Your Pups

Matthew With American Molossus pup

Julianni with American Molossus pups at 5 weeks old

Suffer the pain of discipline or suffer the pain of regret

-Jim Rohn

This is an important chapter, because this could be your first and last litter at the same time, depending on how well you've prepared. Selecting the finest dogs for breeding, learning all of the secrets and techniques will put you on the right track, but selecting the right people and families for these new babies can be difficult! Helping potential buyers find you can be a daunting task as well.

Let's start with selecting a marketing plan that makes you visible and lets people know that you have puppies available. There are several ways to do this and it starts when you have decided to breed a pair. Promoting the breeding should start right then. It gives you 1 to 6 months to get the word out. If you have gone through the selective process, have two great specimens that will make a great pairing for health, function and aesthetics, then why not be proud and promote it? How? Start with your local newspaper, website, Craigslist, online puppy ads, and social media. Believe me; you can't start too early, especially if you aren't a well-established breeder. You must promote and advertize the breeding from the time the decision is made to the time the pregnancy is confirmed via ultrasound or x-ray.

Once pregnancy is confirmed, you can begin accepting deposits. Deposits should always remain in a separate bank account and never spent, in case anything should go wrong. Continue to promote during the entire process till the puppies are born and all are spoken for.

Selecting the right people and families for these wonderful dogs should be a high priority and vetting must be done thoroughly. All dogs were designed by man for specific functions, and all dogs aren't the right fit for everyone. So, make sure to ask lots of questions. This can best be accomplished by developing, or adopting, a questionnaire you can have them fill out. It's important that all the hard work you put into this is rewarded with happy puppies placed in families whose needs are a perfect match for them.

In every case you should be working for a win, win situation, so do your due diligence.

Chapter 10

Be Great

Yvette with Elleganza Della Vecchia Roma 1st place at 9 months

"THE DON" Champion Old World Don Vito and I

No one has ever achieved greatness without dreams

-Roy T Bennett

The goal with this book was to share with you some insight to my perspective on dog breeding. I wanted to share the breeds I love and to give you some helpful information on dog breeding, the whole process. I had a desire to share what to think about, to help you decide if you should or shouldn't, and to inform you about what to expect. Most importantly, however, I wanted this book to help you in life. I want you to understand that you can do anything you want in life. You can achieve anything, once you set your mind to doing so. Create a definite purpose, make a goal, write it down, believe in yourself, and work hard! Take massive action towards that goal; be relentless at it, till you're a success. Dog breeding may, or not, be for you, after reading this book. Regardless, whatever it is you do in life, have passion. Desire to be great, and follow your course with the end in mind. Think in terms of a future eulogy written about you. What will be said about you and your accomplishments? May God bless your endeavors.

Old World Luciana at 6 months with owners
Brint Gurung and Gloria Ruiz

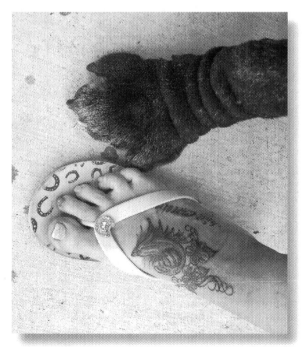

paw of Old World Mr She and owner Merredith Jones

American Molossus Pup Old World Euphrates
with J. Howser of Dark Mountain Mastiffs

Old World Roman owned by Ted Young

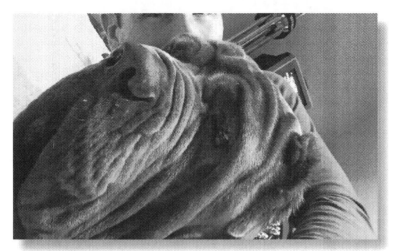

Old World Domiano with owner and Fitness Guru Peter N Nielsen

Old World Constanzia with owner and Fitness Guru Peter N Nielsen

American Molossus puppy Old World Zeba with
Owners Chip Lally and Jaime McCorkindale

Old World Zorah owned by Robin Elysee Jr

Old World Future owned by Bishops K9 Camp

Old World Mickey with owner David Bradley

American Molossus puppy Old World Sheeba with owner Julio Garcia

Old World Dionysus owned by Colonel Daniel Dant and Daina Dant

Old World Cleopatra owned by Diana Knowles of Hotskwash.com

Old World Ren Owned by Steve and Alana
Kendall of West Coast Mastinos

I would like to give special thanks to God, my beautiful wife Yvette Curtis, all of my amazing children, my parents, my grandparents, all our friends, clients, affiliates and fans World Wide. To all the people along the way that helped mentor me, who have worked with me, who have guided me, who have supported me and have been a positive influence in my life. All that I have done and this book couldn't have been possible without you. I also want to thank you personally for purchasing this book. I'm honored and hope you truly enjoy it and receive great value from its contents.

God bless,
Marcus E Curtis

Printed in the United States
By Bookmasters